THE QUEST AND THE QALANDAR
CONVERSATIONS WITH WAQAR FAIZ QALANDAR

First Edition

As told by Waqar Faiz

Transcribed by Omair Shariff

Published by Red Dome Publishing in the USA
www.faizi.org
Copyright © 2021 Omair Shariff
Edited by Ana Joldes
Book illustrated and designed art by Garry Nguyen

TABLE OF CONTENTS

You can say everything is one, but the Divine prefers, "There is nothing but the One!"

FOREWORD

WHAT IS SUFISM?

Much can be said of the word "Sufism." It has become something of a loaded term in our time. The masters of Sufism often remark that Sufism was once a reality without a name, whereas now it is becoming a name without a reality. This means that trying to define Sufism would be to limit it without understanding it. In order to understand it, however, one must experience it.

Sufism is a path that has been laid down by Nabi Pak Muhammad ﷺ, the last and final messenger of the Divine. It is the culmination of the experiences of all the previous prophets and messengers. What this path brings to you is a glimpse of what they brought to their people in their times.

This path is a way of life that enables one to connect to one's Creator. After Nabi Pak Muhammad ﷺ, the inner secrets of this path were first largely conveyed to others by Hazrat Ali, his cousin and son-in-law. This is why Hazrat Ali is known as the Penultimate Master of Sufism. The Sufi path is a living path that continues to this day, brought to the people by the saints of this path, better known as the friends of the Divine (awliya Allah).This inner experience and connection to the Divine have never ceased to be passed from heart to heart. It is for this reason that the cardinal rule of Sufism is that one must find a guide to initiate him into this connection and guide him through the path.

Sufism is the path of Divine friendship. It seeks to bring about the realization that the Divine presence is very close—both to the seeker and to creation as a whole. Instead of focusing solely on the self, the Sufi path aims to negate the self and focus on friendship with the Divine.

The people who have pursued this path have witnessed the love of the Divine unfold in their lives and surroundings.

Instead of defining Sufism, this work aims to highlight key aspects of this path that will allow the reader to get a feel of what its experience may be like. Most importantly, the topics covered are done so through discussion between a guide and his students, the same heart-to-heart format that is the cornerstone of the Sufi path.

TWO FRIENDS MEET WITHIN
TIME. THE DIVINE MEETS
HIS FRIENDS BEYOND TIME.

YOU WILL LEARN TO
OVERLOOK WHEN
MERCY PREVAILS OVER
EVERYTHING YOU SEE.

THE HEART IS NOT
TOUCHED BY WORDS. IT
IS TOUCHED BY THE ONE
WHO UTTERS THEM.

SOMETIMES YOU WILL
MEET HIM, AND YOU WILL
NEVER KNOW. THOSE
ARE THE TIMES IN WHICH
FRIENDSHIP OCCURS.

BECOME THE EYES OF THAT
LIGHT WHOSE VERY SIGHT
PENETRATES THE HEART.

WITH YOUR SURRENDER
BEGINS HIS COMMAND.

SOME LOOKED FOR
BROKEN HEARTS IN ORDER
TO SEARCH FOR HIM.
SOME HAD THEIR OWN
HEARTS BROKEN AS
EXCUSES TO FIND HIM.

BE ONE OF THE FEW
THAT SAY, "I SEEK YOU
BEYOND ANY BLESSING."

YOUR SEARCH BEGINS
WHEN YOU FORM A PLAN.
YOUR JOURNEY BEGINS
WHEN YOU LEARN THAT
THERE IS NO PLAN.

SOMETIMES YOU CALL OUTTO HIM. THIS IS PRAYER. SOMETIMES HE CALLS OUT TO YOU. THIS IS GNOSIS.

THE GOALS OF THIS
WORLD WILL ALWAYS
HAVE OBSTACLES IF YOUR
GOAL IS THE WORLD.

No matter how close
you are, you are
never close enough.

INTRODUCTION

Where can I go to fill this chalice?
To whom do I go to mend this soul?
To cleanse this being of sadness and malice?
How do I reach the ultimate goal?

A thirst for spirituality pervades human consciousness. The passage of time only increases this desire as the people themselves grow increasingly restless. They set out in search of what will make them complete. This is the quest.

A group of some such people once found themselves together and bonded over their mutual longing for that indescribable objective. Though they had found each other, they had not found their goal. They were unsure of where to look, unsure of where to go. They consulted people and attended lectures, but the answers to their questions did little to satisfy them. At times they felt like giving up, and yet they could not deny what they felt within themselves. Just when they thought their anguish would never end, they happened upon a group of people sitting together in discussion. One person among them began to speak. They could tell instantly that this was the leader of the group.

He said:
"Spirituality comes from the soul. The soul, compared to this physical life, experiences neither birth nor death. The life of our physical

body is a dress we wear that can change at any time, but the soul is forever and eternal."

Their bodies froze in shock as their hearts jumped for joy. They felt an ineffable weight behind these words, and they instinctively knew that this was exactly what they had been seeking all this time.

He continued:

"The question is what the state of our soul will be once our physical bodies experience death. The answer to this question is found in this life. Whatever strength we can give to our soul in this life is the state our soul will remain in for eternity. Many people have come before us, and they, too, had to move on from this world. Many will come after us, and they, too, will have to leave. In the end, the soul is what remains forever.

"So, in this physical reality, in order to give strength to our soul and allow it to heal from our inner illnesses, we must work on our spirituality." The group of seekers had heard enough. They sat down with this circle of people and joined the discussion.

They asked:
"How does one work on one's spirituality? What is it that we have been missing?"

The man smiled and said:
"There are many ways to strengthen one's soul, but the component that is missing from you is remembrance of the Divine!"

Puzzled, they asked:
"What does the Divine have to do with spirituality?"

He replied:
"The Divine is the Creator, the One who created you and me, the One who created our souls and blew them into us with such care and attention that has never been shown to any other creature! Always remember, the journey of our soul arriving in this world, transcending the physical nature of this word, and returning to where it came from is entirely and only made possible with the Divine light, the Almighty. The Almighty is the one who made our physical body and then breathed a soul within us. Thereafter, He gave to it a reality that is everlasting. Then, He gave us free will and told us what is right and

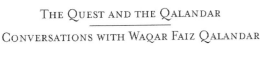
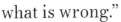
what is wrong."

They asked:
"What does one do with this soul and free will?"

He replied:
"We use that will to choose to follow the Divine Order. The Creator keeps track of each right and wrong decision we make without objection, like an examiner. What will ultimately return to us from this exam is the result of our own doing. Therefore, to keep the result of this test positive, we have to work on our soul."

They asked:
"Spirituality is to choose right over wrong?"

He smiled and said:
"Spirituality is to be human."

They said: "Humans make their own choices without following any order."

He recited the following poem in reply:

Through the ranks of men, I searched far and wide. Yet no human among them could I find.

He continued:

"There is a difference between a human being and being human! Within yourself, there is a war taking place between the soul and the self. When the soul is weak, the self overpowers the soul and controls the body according to its own selfish desires. When the soul is strong, it is operated in singularity and in accordance with the Divine Order."

These seekers, weary from their quest yet intrigued by the words of this unassuming man, searched within themselves in that moment and found his words to ring true. They were beginning to sense that somehow the end of some part of their quest might be at hand. This feeling gave rise to even more questions.

They asked:

"What is the ultimate goal of spirituality?"

He replied:

"To reach the Divine, the One who created the souls we so long to strengthen."

They asked:

How does one reach the Divine?"

He answered:

"One cannot reach the Divine on one's own, but the Divine always ensures that you have a means to reach Him."

They asked:

"What is that means?"

He answered:

"Those who have already reached Him help others reach Him in a chain of masters that goes to the Penultimate Master of our path, the path of Sufism. That Penultimate Master is Hazrat Ali, and from him, the chain goes to the founder of Sufism, Muhammad, the Beloved Messenger of God ﷺ."

At that point, the man excused himself to address some other members of that gathering. The group of seekers found out that this man was Waqar Faiz, a Murshid, a Sufi master, the Qalandar, and that the people gathered in that meeting were his students, seekers like them in quest of the Divine.

When they found some time to speak with him again, they asked:
"What is a Qalandar?"

He laughed softly and said:
"Remember what we said before: there is no death for the soul. The soul is a reality, and this world is nothing but a test. If you are able to strengthen your soul and progress spiritually, the soul is able to come into your own command, for at that point, in your contentment and command lies the contentment and command of the One True Light. Suffice it to say for now that the one who has truly mastered this is able to comprehend the stage of the Qalandar, the one who has a direct connection with the Penultimate Master Hazrat Ali!"

With these words, the seekers knew that they had found more than what they were looking for. They were convinced that the man who sat before them was the one who would complete their quest. They pledged themselves to Murshid Waqar Faiz Qalandar and became his students. Their search was finally over, but their journey had just begun.

This book is composed of conversations like the one above between seekers on this quest and Murshid Waqar Faiz, the master who guides them on it. They contain information about some aspects of the spiritual path for those who are curious and offer insight for fellow seekers. This is The Quest and the Qalandar.

ON THE SPIRITUAL PATH,
YOU WILL GET WHAT YOU
WANT. SOME SETTLE FOR
THINGS, BUT ONLY A FEW
WILL SETTLE FOR THE ONE
WHO MADE EVERYTHING.

THE FIRST DIALOGUE

SLEEP AND WAKEFULNESS

A few students were once seated with the Qalandar, and their meeting extended into the long hours of the night. They sat in silence for some time until he said: "These are the moments in which the Divine speaks to the human heart. In the dead of the night, while we are asleep, He calls out to us."

A student asked:
"What does He say?"

He smiled and said:
"He says, 'Worship is better than sleep.'"

Another student asked:
"Why is it that we don't hear this call?"

He replied:

"Some cannot hear it, some do not heed it, some heed it without hearing it, and some always hear it. This last group is composed of those people who are in a state of worship even while sleeping."

Another student asked:

"If they are in a state of worship while sleeping, why do they awaken for worship at all? Isn't their sleep better than worship?"

The master replied:

"There are three stages of human worship. The first stage is a stage of complete unawareness. It is the sleep of the heart that is akin to death. The heart gives no attention to the Divine. In this stage, your body is alive, but the heart feels dead within. This is the stage of the living dead. People whose hearts are this way can neither hear the call nor heed it

"The second stage is a stage of heeding the call. A person forces himself to wake up and devote his time to worship and bow his head in submission to his Lord. The heart begins to gain life in this stage, but the person worshiping is still in a state

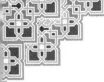

of doubt. He doubts whether his worship is seen by the Divine."

A student asked:

"How can one reach the second stage if one does not hear the call? How can one heed the call if one cannot hear it?"

He replied:

"This is the work of the spiritual guide. It is the guide who informs the seekers of this call to the Divine, just as we have informed you this very night. It is the guide who enlivens the heart of the seeker and prepares it for a state of worship. Once the seeker is made aware of the call, he begins to heed it, even though he does not hear it."

He continued:

"The third stage is a stage of complete awareness. By constantly devoting time to his worship, a person's heart becomes completely alive, and he becomes closer to the Divine. This is true wakefulness. Now, even his sleep becomes a form of worship, and his worship becomes his ascension. This seeker is one of those who always hear the call.

"At this stage, a person calls out the to the Divine, and the Divine answers him. He reaches such a point of surety in the Divine that the Divine regards it with love and says, 'You have not even seen Me, yet you still believe in Me. Now, I will personally respond to you.' Such a person has removed all layers of doubt from his heart, allowing only the light of the Creator to enter and remain. When a person reaches this stage and chooses with his own will to awaken for worship and switch from one form of worship to another, he will taste the reality of worship being better than sleep. That is why my master Hazrat Ali says, 'I have never worshiped Him without seeing Him.'"

A TRUE FIRST STEP
IS ONE WHERE YOU
DON'T STEP BACK.

THE SECOND DIALOGUE

DIVINE CHARACTER

Some students once came to visit the revered master. A student asked: Is it possible to be like the Divine?

He replied:

"To even imagine what the Divine Essence is like is impossible. However, there are those who reach such a state that they see no one and nothing other than Him, even when they look to themselves."

Another student asked:

"How can one reach that stage?"

He replied:

"The starting point for such people was that they began by emulating the character of the Divine."

The student asked:

"What is the character of the Divine?"

He smiled and said:

"He is the Most Compassionate, the Most Merciful."He continued: "The ones who reach this stage are none other than the friends of the Divine. The Almighty has accorded them a status such that their burial places are extensions of His noble court. In these places, you will find people from all corners of the globe and all walks of life. They find spiritual solace in these places because these friends of the Divine devoted their lives to the Divine Character, the character of compassion and empathy.

"A human without empathy is like a walking corpse, and a soul without compassion will always remain thirsty. Those whose hearts are chained to the attachments of the world can never experience the freedom of mercy and compassion.

"The ultimate example of compassion and mercy is found in the founder of Sufism, Nabi Pak Muhammad ﷺ. There are many instances in which he showcased the compassion and mercy of the Divine. Once, the child of one of his companions had gone missing, and so the companion came to the Noble Nabi for help. During their conversation, a man arrived and informed him that his child was happily playing with other children in a nearby garden. The companion rushed to take his child, but the Noble Nabi stopped him and said, 'Make sure when you call to your child in the garden, do not address him as "my child" or 'my son.'"

The companion asked:
"Why not, o Noble Nabi?"

He replied:
"It could be one of the children he is playing with is an orphan and has no father, and upon hearing you say this, he might feel an emptiness in his heart. You would not want a child to feel that he is missing something.

"So, the compassion of the Creator is not found in the things that we do. Rather, the compassion

11

of the Creator is found in the feelings that are hidden behind our actions. This emulation of Divine Character takes us from the apparent to the hidden, and this is where the Creator is found."

I SHARED WITH HIM THE SECRETS OF MY LIFE. HE SHARED WITH ME THE SECRETS OF ETERNITY.

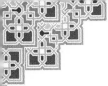

THE THIRD DIALOGUE

FRIENDSHIP

Some students were once seated with the master, and they asked him about the spiritual path.

One of them said:

"What exactly is the goal of this path? What does it mean to find the Divine?"

He replied:

"The goal is indeed to find the Divine, and the meaning of finding the Divine is forming a friendship with the Divine. This is the path of Divine friendship."

Another student asked:

"What does it mean to be a friend of the Divine?"

He said:

"Let me ask any of you what you think friendship with Him is."

One of them said:

"He is the One who protected us from harm and hurt. He is the only one who loves us unconditionally. We always find Him next to us. He does everything for us without proclaiming what He has done, and He does it unconditionally."

Another student said:

"The world constantly attacks the spiritual traveler and tries to weaken him with every step. The Divine shows us His friendship by delivering us from that harm and allowing us to continue on the path that leads to Him."

The venerable master paused for a moment and said:

"These are all the ways in which the Divine shows love to us. He loves more than seventy mothers. Friendship, however, is not like motherhood.

Friendship is a two-way street. You have mentioned some great examples of His love for us, but have you ever considered these examples and thought about how close He is to you and how far you are from Him?"

He continued:

"Some of us live in a shallow world where we have never encountered the love of a true friend. Some of us live in an even shallower world where we, having encountered that friend and having experienced that love, fail to connect to him at a similar level.

"Yes, the Divine protects us from physical and spiritual harm, and He nurtures our physical and spiritual growth. However, these things are all associated with our own interests, our own selves. The essence of friendship is to move beyond our own selves and look to the Divine Self. The Divine makes sure we wake up to a new day but have any of us ever called out to Him and asked, 'How are you today?'

"Friendship is made with the Divine Essence, not the Attributes. We note a few of His Attributes, His Compassion, Mercy, Love, and so on, and we think that these Attributes are the same as the Divine. The truth is that we experience these Attributes, we experience what He offers, and we stop there, failing to connect with Him as an entity."

One student asked:

"If friendship is made with the Essence and not the Attributes, then why mention the Attributes at all?"

He smiled and said:

"The point of mentioning them is so that we can understand that the Divine is not just a concept. He is an actual entity with thoughts and feelings, though they are not like ours. Once we are given an understanding of the Divine Nature, then we can actually hope to connect with Him on a deeper level."

Another student asked:

"How does one gain this understanding?"

He replied:

"How do you usually make friends with someone you have never seen or heard of before? One of that person's friends whom you do know introduces you. Similarly, those who are already friends of the Divine introduce others to the Divine. Your gateway to the Divine will always be through the ones that He loves. They are the ones who convey that understanding to others, from heart to heart."

The same student asked:

"After being given that understanding, how does one connect to the Divine in this way?"

He smiled and said:

"You do not find Divine love. Divine Love finds you. All you have to do is remain loyal to the one who is already His friend, and Divine friendship will envelop you. After being in the company with one engrossed in the perspective of the Divine, you yourself will start to perceive that perspective. On this path, you start the process, and He completes it for you. This is friendship at its purest and best."

He continued:

"A seeker starts this path experiencing the Divine Attributes only for himself. As he continues his journey, he starts witnessing those Attributes affect others. He perceives the Attributes of the

Divine resonating throughout creation. This is the start of a friendship with the Divine. It is the Almighty unveiling His secrets to you. You start to see what He likes and dislikes. As this understanding grows deeper, the Divine begins to unveil Himself to you until you are no longer looking at Him as distant from you; rather, you will experience Him alongside you. At this point, you will cease to see things from your perspective, and you will begin to see things from the Divine's perspective. This is when the Divine unveils His Essence to you, for the only one who can look to the Divine Essence is the Divine Himself. This is the point where two friends meet each other as one. This connection can only be experienced in the presence of someone who already has this connection, and so this is what the spiritual guide gives to you from his heart to yours."

SUBMISSION IS A MATTER OF HOW DEEP YOU TAKE YOUR LOVE. THE DEEPER YOUR LOVE, THE GREATER YOU WILL SUBMIT. THE SIGN OF YOUR LOVE FOR THE CREATOR IS YOUR LEVEL OF SUBMISSION TO HIM.

THE FOURTH DIALOGUE

SUBMISSION

Some students once asked the Qalandar about the nature of the spiritual path.

He said:

"The path itself has layers of depth. There is a path to friendship, a path to loyalty, and a path to ˉishq. The nature of the spiritual path will depend on what level of depth your path has taken."

One of the students asked:

"Isn't ˉishq just love? Why is that its own path when love is required for both friendship and loyalty? Isn't love required throughout the path?"

He replied:

"Love is the root of this path, yes. However, ˈishq is not the same as love. The difference between ˈishq and love is as the difference between the sky and the earth. When you love a person and say, 'I love you,' you will get angry when he doesn't say, 'I love you' back. When you have ˈishq and say, 'I love you,' you don't care about the response. Love is an emotion. ˈIshq is a state of the heart and soul that pervades your very being. Love can be easily misrepresented. ˈIshq can hardly be understood. Love can come and go. ˈIshq is a constant presence that fuels your ascension. Love can be easily dismissed. ˈIshq is something that will burn everything around it without the one that has it becoming burned himself. Love is limited. ˈIshq is unlimited, like the Creator Himself. This is why the level of ˈishq is the deepest level of this path."

Another student asked:

"What is the nature of the path when it takes on this level of depth?"

He replied:

"The deeper the level, the greater the test. Just

as every day is a new day, every day will bring a new trial."

Another student asked:
"How does one overcome these trials?"

He said:
"The key to overcoming these trials and deepening one's path at the same time is to do one act again and again: submission."

He continued:
"Just as the path has levels of depth, so too does submission. The first level of submission is the submission required to be on this path. It is the acceptance of the Divine and of the masters of this path, namely the founder of Sufism the Messenger Muhammad ﷺ, the Penultimate Master Ali, and one's own spiritual guide. With this submission, one is truly ready to begin spiritual development.

"The next level of submission is the submission of friendship. It is the acceptance of His love in your life. That Divine Love frees you from need and liberates you to a degree from the clutches of worldly desire.

"The next level is that of loyalty. Having attained a degree of freedom from the desire for the material world, the world will seek to chase after you and offer itself up to you. Everyone tries to chase after the world, and it evades their grasp, yet this same world spreads itself out at the doorsteps of the friends of the Divine, but they never accept it."

A student said:

"They say that when the Divine loves you, He bestows you with worldly pleasures."

He smiled and replied:

"I have heard the Divine Himself say that He loves you even more when, after receiving those pleasures, you look to Him and say, 'I leave these pleasures for You.' This is the submission of loyalty. The person at this stage has made his heart an abode for the Divine. How can such a person dare to let something or someone else step in? The moment something else steps in, the Divine leaves, and when He leaves, nothing remains."

He continued:

"The final level of submission is that of ⁻ishq. At this stage, the seeker turns away not only from the material world but also from the spiritual world, making his only object of focus the Almighty. At this point, he no longer has any goal or objective. Every act of submission done at this level opens up new perspectives of the Divine to him."

Another student asked:

"These acts of submission can be done more than once?"

He replied:

"These acts of submission are done several times at every level. "The world once tried to come to me. It told me how precious I was to it and how it could offer me what most people could only dream of. It was easy enough to turn away, but there was still a question about the world in my heart. In that moment, I turned to the Almighty and asked, 'Why is the world chasing after me when I do not need it? Why is it trying to find a place in my heart when I have already submitted my very being to You?'

"He replied, 'Every time it comes to you, it is you who must make a choice to accept it or reject it. When people say they surrender, how much are they truly willing to relinquish? Are they willing to simply give up worldly pleasures, or are they willing to give up their very existence to Me? This is the ultimate choice they must make, and everything else will revolve around this decision.'"

"That day, the true meaning of absolute submission was unveiled to me. Letting go of the world for His sake is one thing, but letting go of yourself along with your desires, the world, and its pleasures is another. The first is loyalty. The second is ‾ishq.

"Someone at the level of ‾ishq has made his heart a perfect abode for the Divine; who else can share that space with Him? At that point, anything other than Him becomes a trial and a test."

Another student asked:
"Is there a point where these trials end?"

He smiled and replied:
"Someone at the level of ‾ishq actually enjoys the

trials and struggles. This is the meaning behind the Divine's statement, 'Those who surrender their will to Me suffer neither pain nor regret.'"

He paused, looked away for a moment, chuckled softly, and said:

"There is actually a secret stage beyond this that only a few of the closest friends of the Divine are privy to. At the stage of ⁻ishq, one becomes an ardent lover of the Divine, subject to the beloved's trials and tests. There is a stage beyond this, however, where the Divine becomes the ardent lover, and the seeker becomes the beloved. At this stage, everything is turned on its head. Here, the beloved finds the Divine by turning away from Him, and indulgence in worldly activities becomes submission. This stage is found only in the rarest of cases and can only be understood by the truly enlightened. The seeker in a state of ⁻ishq could only experience the Divine from one perspective. For the beloved, the experience of the Divine is a reality from every perspective. This is a submission beyond all submissions. It is the beloved's submission to the Creator's ⁻ishq for him.

"Having such a relationship with the Creator

is not meant for everyone, but if people could understand that the Almighty can love a person without any bounds that we can envision, then this would be the ultimate submission for people. It is a submission that can open the doors to His endless secrets in a single night."

SERVICE TO CREATION
IS, IN REALITY, SERVICE
TO THE CREATOR. IF
HE CHOOSES YOU TO BE
THERE FOR HIS PEOPLE, IT
IS A BLESSING FOR YOU.

THE FIFTH DIALOGUE

WHERE DO WE FIND HIS CLOSEST FRIENDS?

The master was once seated in a gathering with some visitors. The topic of the friends of the Divine arose.

A visitor asked:

"Who exactly are the friends of the Divine? How does one recognize them?"

He replied:

"A true friend of the Divine is one who sees everyone except himself as a friend to the Divine."

Another visitor asked:

"Doesn't that mean that every person will offer us

spiritual guidance? Why is it that one must seek out one spiritual guide when one must consider everyone a friend to the Divine?"

He said:

"There are two groups we are speaking of. The first group is friends to the Divine, and the second is friends of the Divine. A seeker will encounter both groups before and after he meets his spiritual guide."

The same visitor asked:

"Who are friends to the Divine? What are some signs of recognizing them?"

He replied:

"Friends to the Divine are found anywhere and everywhere. They are not determined by their wealth, clothing, speech, or status. They are determined purely by the Divine Alone. If there were any one sign of recognizing a friend to the Divine, it would be that the Divine is found with those who are brokenhearted. When the Divine enters the heart of a brokenhearted person, he becomes a wellspring of wisdom for those around him without realizing it himself. He will be focused on his grief, while the Divine will speak through him to others and provide morsels of guidance to people, regardless of whether they are walking the spiritual path or not. Just as the Almighty provides physical sustenance to people through food and water, he provides spiritual sustenance to people as well, and this is His system."

Another visitor asked:
"Why is grief the channel for this spiritual sustenance? Why isn't it any other emotion?"

He replied:
"Attraction to the world is one of the four great enemies of mankind. Each human being has necessities and a purpose. Our necessities are found in this world, but our purpose is found beyond it. We confuse the necessities of life for our purpose in life, and so the world and its attractions distract us from our true priorities. The world, however, is innately disloyal, and it will never fulfill our expectations. When these expectations break, so too do our hearts, and the Divine will always unveil His presence in those moments to provide comfort and solace to those who are grief-stricken and wisdom to those around the grief-stricken who need it."

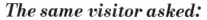
The same visitor asked:
"So, the Divine breaks people's hearts to provide wisdom?"

He replied:
"It is never the Divine who breaks hearts. It is people who break each other's hearts with their own decisions. The Almighty created people to love one another, and He created things to be used by people. The reason many people's lives are empty is that they love things and use people. The Divine will always be a friend to those who encounter such situations."

Another visitor asked:
"What impact do these friends to the Divine have on those who are on the spiritual path?"

He replied:
"Friends to the Divine provide moments of guidance to those people searching for the path and reminders to those who are traveling the path."

The same visitor asked:
"Can a friend to the Divine properly guide a

person on the path?"

He replied:

"No. Friends to the Divine provide moments of clarity and wisdom, but they are not even aware of their own spiritual states, let alone the states of others. They do not actively call people toward the Divine and have no knowledge of the path and its intricacies. In order to start the path and travel it, one must find an actual friend of the Divine.

"Like friends to the Divine, friends of the Divine have no outward signs, and they do not conform to any ideal or standard that we presuppose. However, the difference between the two groups is huge. Friends to the Divine have had their hearts broken by the world. Friends of the Divine have turned away from the world and surrendered their hearts to their Creator. Friends to the Divine have a deep yet temporary link with the Almighty. Friends of the Divine are constantly linked to Him in this way through a chain of spiritual masters. Friends to the Divine are hardly aware of His presence. Friends of the Divine perceive nothing but His presence. It is the friends of the Divine who invite others and introduce them to the Divine Essence. These are the close friends of the Almighty whom one must seek out if one desires to walk the spiritual path."

Another visitor asked:

"If it is so necessary to find one of these friends, and if there are no outward signs, how does one find a friend of the Divine?"

He replied:

"The guidance that the Divine provides through friends to the Divine will eventually lead you to a friend of the Divine."

The same visitor said:

"There are many who go out in search of such a friend, but they claim they could not find anyone to guide them."

He replied:

"This path is determined by the purity of one's intention. If there is no purity, then either you will never find that friend, or you will find him in front of you and dismiss him. Many of us have built an image of a friend of the Divine in our minds. We have made criteria based on our own assumptions, and we want His friend to match all of them. We tend to believe that His friends look a certain way, talk a certain way, or live a certain way. So, when we see someone who is actually His friend, we say: 'Let's see whether this person fits my criteria of being a friend of the Divine or not,' and when that someone does not meet those self-made criteria, we dismiss him. All of these assumptions and expectations take us to a point where we fill our hearts with doubts and inflate our egos, and so we are unable to receive true guidance through any of His real friends, saying instead that we tried to seek out one of His friends but could find no one. How can a friend of the Unlimited Divine ever fit into any of our limited criteria?"

The same visitor said:
"There are many people who falsely claim to be guides too, so there must be some way to tell who is real."

He said:
"If your intention to seek the Divine is pure and firmly rooted within your heart, then your heart will tell you who is real and who is not. When you are firm in your intention, then how can your heart not tell you what is real?"

He added:

"If you are pure in your quest, then you will also feel an impact from your encounter with a friend of the Divine. When that special friend of the Divine is encountered, his level of belief will shake you to your core, where something inside of you starts to crack. There is an unseen light that moves into you at that moment because the condition of the heart of that human being you encountered has completely overwhelmed you. At that moment, you come to the realization that it is the Divine, in fact, giving you this light from that heart. Then you come to a point where your soul and heart want to receive from this heart, but your own ego wants to turn away from it. This point only becomes clear for those who have truly sought the Divine. It then becomes the first and last step of your spirituality. After this encounter, you enter into a state of submission in recognition of that special Divine presence."

Another visitor asked:

"Why is it though that only one friend of the Divine can guide you?"

He smiled and said:

"The Almighty is One in every sense of the word. If you want to be guided to the One, then He will guide you to one who will guide you to the One. When the Divine desires to bestow you with something, He will always do so through the hands of people. When He desires to give you something only meant for you, He will do so through the hands of the one who is meant to be your guide. Your relationship with the One starts with one and ends with one. As far as the seeker is concerned, his guide is the closest friend of the Divine."

HOLD ONTO ONE GOOD
THING, ANYTHING, BE IT
BIG OR SMALL, AND STAY
CONSISTENT WITH IT. THIS
IS THE CORE OF YOUR
PATH TO THE DIVINE.

THE SIXTH DIALOGUE

CRUELY & WORSHIP

Some students and visitors were once sitting with the Qalandar, and the discussion turned to the topic of the light of the Divine.

A visitor asked:
"Where is the light of the Divine found?"

He replied:
"The light of the Divine can be found anywhere, but the place it is stored in is the human heart."

The same visitor asked:
"If the light of the Divine is found within us,

doesn't that mean that the Divine Himself is within us?"

Smiling, he shook his head and said:
"Compared to the light of the Divine found with the Divine, the light of the Divine within a heart is like a candle in the face of the Sun. Just because you have the light of the Divine doesn't mean you have the Divine Himself."

A visitor asked:
"I hear many people of spirituality say that everything is within us. If the Divine is not within us, what does this saying mean?"

He replied:
"Everything is definitely within you: everything good as well as everything bad. Only when someone becomes close to the Divine does he cast off the bad and embrace the good."

He continued:
"If the heart is where the light of the Divine manifests, then there must also be a place where all the darknesses of the human being gather. That place is the self."

A student asked:

"How does one define or understand the self?"

He replied:

"A human is composed of two things: the physical and the spiritual. The physical will decay and pass away, but the spiritual will remain forever. That spiritual part of you is the heart and soul, and the physical part is the mind and body—the self. It can also be called the ego, the part of you that is attached to the life of this world."

A visitor asked:

"If the self is the part of you that will pass on, why is it referred to as the self? Shouldn't the self be the part that will remain forever?"

He replied:

"It is called the self because the majority of us make choices that give strength to the physical and neglect the spiritual. We are who we choose to be. This is why the self is one of the four major enemies of man."

A student asked:

"What are some signs to distinguish the presence

of the self?"

He said:

"Just as the heart is the place where love manifests, the self is the place where cruelty manifests, cruelty toward yourself.

"Cruelty is considered to be exploiting or wronging others, but this is, in reality, wronging yourself. People choose to exploit and wrong others because it contains some physical benefit or advantage for themselves, and to choose the physical over the spiritual is the essence of cruelty. It is even worse when one commits such acts in his daily routine but does not even consider what he did to be wrong. These acts put spiritual rust and dirt on the heart that cover the light of the Divine within."

He added:

"Another form of cruelty is linked not to bad deeds, but to good deeds."

A visitor asked:

"How is cruelty done with good deeds?"

He replied:

"It is done when someone does a good deed, but he only does so because he sees some benefit in it. He does not do it to please the Divine but to please his own ego. Now, even spiritual acts are reduced to physical performances, and the spiritual results of your efforts go to waste. This is the ultimate form of cruelty that extinguishes the Divine light in your heart."

A student asked:

"How does one avoid the pitfalls of cruelty?"

He replied:

"Freedom from cruelty is attained by striving to fulfill one's responsibilities to the Divine and His servants."

A visitor asked:

"What are these responsibilities?"

He replied:

"Responsibilities to the Divine center around your conviction that He is the only One worthy of worship. Responsibilities to His servants center around the Activities of the Divine Himself: feeding the hungry, clothing the naked, visiting the sick, etc. Striving to fulfill these responsibilities increases the light of the Divine in the heart. Physical sustenance is found in feeding one's self. Spiritual sustenance is found in feeding others."

Another visitor asked:
"What happens when these two responsibilities clash with each other?"

He replied:
"The reality is that these two will never actually clash, for service to the creation is itself a form of worship."

Another visitor asked:
"What happens if we are unable to fulfill these responsibilities?"

He smiled and said:
"The key is to try. As humans, our only job is to take a step, and completion is the job of the Creator. The Almighty knows best what is in our hearts, and He will bestow light and wisdom according to the intentions of our actions, not their results. Cruelty is found when we do not try at all."

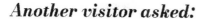

Another visitor asked:

"What should our intention be in such situations?"

He said:

"Worship is always done for the sake of the Divine Alone. He is the One who provides for creation, and if your hands are the ones that are giving in His Name, then it is a blessing for you. He will fulfill those needs with or without you. If you put people in the forefront and forget about the Divine, then it no longer becomes worship but just another form of cruelty. Cruelty and worship will always be at odds with each other, just like the self and the soul."

A student asked:

"What is the best form of worship?"

He replied:

"The best form of worship is charity, and the best charity is to forgive others. This will not only end cruelty in yourself but cruelty in others as well."

A visitor asked:

"How does forgiving others end their cruelty?"

He said:

"The Almighty Himself says, 'My Mercy predominates My Wrath.' Forgiveness is also an Activity of the Divine. Just as engaging in the other Activities of the Divine causes His light to shine and descend within us, so too does engaging in this act. When one engages in charity, for example, the Divine does not discriminate between the giver and the receiver. Both receive His light equally. Forgiveness is the same way."

Another visitor said:

"What you just said seems like too big of a task for some of us."

He laughed softly and said:

"We definitely cannot do big things every day, but we can do small things with a lot of love and care. Start with something small, but do it with a lot of love, and the Creator will accept it. His acceptance will open your heart to greater acts."

A student asked:

"What is the worship and cruelty of a Sufi?"

He replied:

"A Sufi is someone who has been bestowed with a lot of light and wisdom by the Creator. Depending on his duty, he will either remain engrossed in that light or pass it on to others. If he does not remain engrossed in that light, or if he avoids passing it on to others, then that would be his cruelty."

Another student asked:

"What is the worship of a friend of the Divine?"

He said:

"A friend of the Divine is one who reminds others of the Divine. His duty is to bring about worship in others and to remove cruelty from them. He reminds others that we shall all end and return to our Creator. He prepares others to meet their Creator in a good state, reminding them that this life will end, but our actions and their consequences, good or ill, will last forever."

Conversations with Waqar Faiz Qalandar

HE WAITS FOR YOU TO
TURN BACK TO HIM
EVERY TIME YOU MAKE A
MISTAKE. ONE MISTAKE
AND ONE REPENTANCE
TAKE YOU CLOSER TO THE
ONE THAN A THOUSAND
DAYS OF WORSHIP.

THE SEVENTH DIALOGUE

LIFE & ETERNAL LIFE

While seated in a gathering, a student once asked the Qalandar: "What is life?"

The venerable master replied:
"Death."

Perplexed, the student then asked:
"Then what is death?"

He said: "Life."

Seeing the looks of consternation on the faces of the students and visitors, he chuckled softly and said:

"Life has three degrees: death, true life, and eternal life. To understand the degrees of life, we must first understand Divine Love."

He continued:

"The Almighty once revealed to David that when His servants turn away from Him, He awaits their return with so much intensity that if the sons of Adam knew, they would tear themselves to shreds. This is the story of human life. We err, He awaits. We return, He forgives. Life is nothing but a series of errors, yet that Divine Love causes each error to become a means of drawing closer to Him."

A visitor asked:

"Why is human life always expressed as mistakes and sins? Why are we always being told that we are doing wrong?"

He replied:

"This life has been given as a gift to us. It is an opportunity to draw nearer to Him than any other creation. Every human being will have experienced the presence of the Divine at some point in his or her life. That test you didn't study for yet passed because of some surprise extra credit—that was Allah. The extra money you got in the mail at the exact time of need—that was Allah. People receiving something to eat despite not having the ability to buy their own food—that is Allah. Any experience in which you needed something and survived was Allah. The question is: Are we paying attention? Did we heed the signs? Did we try to draw closer to that presence we felt? If we look deep within ourselves, we will find that, for the majority of our lives, we did not. To express a lifestyle characterized by choices that lead us away from our Creator as sinful is a mercy; it would be more accurate to express it as death."

Another visitor asked:

"If the Divine loves us so much and shows His presence in our lives this way, then what about the bad things that happen to people? Why do we lose loved ones? Why are innocent people taken by diseases?"

He replied:

"These things happen as a mercy, too. They are reminders that we cannot live this life according to our desires, nor can we dictate the outcomes of our affairs. The reality is that every other person we lay eyes on has the mentality of Pharaoh. The only difference is that Allah did not give them the kind of power that was given to Pharaoh. If everything happened according to how we wanted, we would surely forget about the Divine presence and attribute divinity to ourselves as Pharaoh did. So, these things happen so that we know that there is only one Creator in absolute control, and the people whose lives are ended in this way are given a special status in the Afterlife, the life that will last forever."

Another visitor asked:
"Why is the Afterlife given so much importance on this path?"

He replied:
"The Afterlife is the completion of that basic Divine love that is shown to humanity. Every human being has a connection with the Divine, and one can actualize that connection following a spiritual path as well. The question, however, is whether this actualized connection will last forever. If it does not last forever, then that is death, for there is no clearer definition of death than the ending of that connection. If it does last forever, then this is true life. The only way that

it will last, however, is if it lasts beyond one's physical death, the point where the life of the Afterlife begins. The Afterlife, then, is the place where true life finds its completion, and its start is found at the acceptance of this path of the Afterlife, the path of Nabi Pak Muhammad ﷺ."

A student asked:
"Is the Afterlife the same as eternal life?"

He replied:
"The Afterlife is certainly everlasting, but eternal life can be found even before the Afterlife. Eternal life is realized when one submits himself completely to the Will of the Divine."

A student asked:
"Does eternal life mean that a person will stop making mistakes?"

He replied:
"Angels are beings that can commit no sin. Humans make mistakes all the time, yet they are considered far superior to angels. To call a human being an angel is nothing short of an insult. The Will of the Divine is that we remain

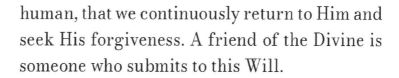

human, that we continuously return to Him and seek His forgiveness. A friend of the Divine is someone who submits to this Will.

"Let me share an incident of one such friend of the Almighty. He was once a king who lived a lavish lifestyle and gave it up in his quest for the Divine. His quest took him to the Ka῾ba in Mecca, and there he harbored a secret desire to circle the Ka῾ba alone without any other worshippers. One night it rained heavily, and so no worshippers came out to circle the Ka῾ba. He found that moment he was longing for. As he began circling the Ka῾ba, he started praying, 'O Allah, save me from sin, O Allah save me from sin.' He continued to make this supplication while circling the Ka῾ba until he suddenly heard a voice call to him, 'Everyone asks that I save them from sin. If I save you too, then how will anyone know that I am the Most Forgiving, the Most Merciful?'

"So, the friends of the Divine submit to this Will of His, and in exchange, they draw closer to the Divine than others. They eventually reach a state where the Divine light envelops them so much that they are shielded from a state of wrongdoing. This state is the start of eternal life, and it is only in this state of eternal life that one can carry out the Work of the Divine. This is why the Divine entrusts His Work to His friends, for He has already entrusted His Will to them, and they, in turn, have accepted it fully."

A visitor asked:
"What is the point of all of these stages? Why is it that the Creator has hidden Himself from us in this life?"

He replied: "For the people of death, it is for the trial of their acceptance of the Divine. Trials are opportunities for drawing closer to Him, and it is the way for them to reciprocate the love given to them by the Divine. For the people of true life, it is to pay the reward for their faith to the fullest, for the reward given in the Afterlife is one that will last forever. For the people of eternal life, it is to keep the fire of their ¯ishq alive. An ardent lover has no greater desire than to stay in the longing to see his beloved. If the Creator were to show Himself to them now, that desire would no longer remain, and they would lose that state of ¯ishq."

Another visitor asked:

"Isn't the Afterlife just Heaven and Hell? I thought the Sufi was supposed to look beyond those things."

He smiled and said:

"The Afterlife is more than just Heaven and Hell. Yes, those who had desires in this life will have them fulfilled in the Afterlife, but those who had only the desire to see their Creator will remain with Him, and the Creator does not exist within the bounds of Heaven. The Creator will make sure everyone who accepted this path and took it on will be satisfied; for some, it will mean fulfilling desires and keeping them in Heaven. For the friends of the Divine, it will mean setting them aside just for Himself."

A student asked:

"What is the pinnacle of eternal life?"

He replied:

"The pinnacle of eternal life is when one's very soul is taken to the Afterlife while the physical body is still alive, and that physical body is filled with nothing but the Divine light."

He paused for a moment and continued:

"Many of us see the souls of the departed friends of the Divine in dreams or meditations. Some can see their souls with their waking eyes. Have you ever asked why they are seen here on this earth when they can go anywhere else? Their graves are palaces both physically and in the realm of the unseen. They can cross into any world they like, just like any of us cross over a river. Why is it that they are here then? It is because the Divine is found here. They searched the cosmos and found nothing, they searched the unseen realm and found nothing, yet here they find everything. The Divine is found here, and anyone who realizes this fact during his life on this earth has uncovered the deepest secret to eternal life."

EVERYTHING POSITIVE AND
NEGATIVE IS WITHIN YOU.
WHAT YOU SEE OUTSIDE
IS ONLY A REFLECTION
OF YOUR INNER SELF.
POSITIVITY WILL ALWAYS
LEAD YOU TO HIM,
AND NEGATIVITY WILL
EVENTUALLY LEAD YOU
TO SELF-DESTRUCTION.
SO, TAKE A PAUSE,
SILENCE YOUR MIND, AND
LISTEN TO YOUR SOUL.

THE EIGHTH DIALOGUE

POSITIVITY & THE SELF

Murshid was once speaking to a group of students and visitors when one student asked about spiritual enlightenment.

He said:

"Spiritual enlightenment is often considered the pinnacle of spiritual achievement. On this path, however, it is simply a prerequisite to attaining an intimate understanding of the Divine. Enlightenment comes from understanding the self, and the one who knows himself knows his Lord."

A visitor asked:

"How must the self be understood?"

He replied:

The only way to understand it is as an enemy. It is the self that stops you from taking the spiritual path, and it is always the self that holds you back.

"There was once a great friend of the Divine who would call out to Him often. One day he called out, 'O Allah, how do I reach You?' He immediately heard the reply, 'Leave yourself and come!' The spiritual journey is all about leaving behind the things of this world you have accumulated, and the self is the ultimate child of the world."

Another visitor asked:

"How can one fix the self?"

He said:

"The self does not need to be fixed; it needs to be annihilated in the Divine. As long as the self exists, there will always be something inside of yourself that competes with the Almighty. The self is something that always views itself as the best and others as inferior. This is why we jump at chances to get ahead of others and justify decisions we know in our hearts to be wrong."

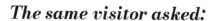
The same visitor asked:
"Then how does one annihilate the self and reach enlightenment?"

He smiled and said:
"Positivity. Positivity is to see yourself as others see you and to see others as you see yourself. It means to see only the good qualities in others and to see only the bad qualities within yourself. It is to assume the best of others in spite of your misgivings and suspicions. If you can remove the negative and embrace the positive, you will attain spiritual enlightenment."

A visitor said:
"Easier said than done."

He smiled and replied:
"If you try to do it by yourself, you will find it impossible. If you have a guide to take you on this path and you give yourself over to him, you will find it very easy. If we cannot understand people, we cannot understand the Creator, and if we cannot submit ourselves to the one that the Divine has kept as our guide, how can we ever hope to submit to Him?"

He continued:

"The self must be annihilated, and yet man cannot annihilate it himself. Only the Divine can annihilate it if the seeker submits himself. This is why the Beloved Nabi Muhammad ﷺ left us a path to follow. Following that path is the first form of submission and the first blow against the self for many people. Positivity leads to spiritual enlightenment and, for many people, it is the second blow against the self. The third blow comes when your Lord is pleased with you. This is the stage where the seeker's emotions fade away and are replaced with an acute awareness of the Divine Attributes."

A student asked:

"What are some signs of spiritual enlightenment?"

He replied:

"The greatest sign is humility. Humility cannot be developed; it must be instilled. The greater one submits in positivity, the greater his humility will be.

"When you walk up a mountain, you bend forward and hunch your shoulders so that you can climb higher. When you walk down the mountain, you stiffen up so as not to slip. Similarly, when you are on an upward journey toward your Creator, you will remain bent and hunched in humility. If you stiffen up in pride, it means you're on the way down."

He continued:

"Positivity itself has levels: positivity toward others, positivity toward the Divine, positivity toward the path, and positivity toward the guide. Positivity toward others we have already discussed. Positivity toward the Divine is basically having a good opinion of the Creator and entrusting Him with your wellbeing, spiritual as well as physical. Positivity toward the path involves accepting the path of Nabi Pak Muhammad ﷺ and Hazrat Ali and staying determined despite any obstacles. The four enemies of mankind will always give you trouble at this level."

A visitor asked:

"What are these four enemies?"

He replied: "The devil, the self, attraction to the world, and bad company. When one is at the level

of positivity toward the path, these enemies will try their very hardest to stop him from moving forward."

He continued:

"Positivity toward the guide is where the self can strike the hardest. It can be a very difficult thing to choose one person to take you on your spiritual journey. The self will always seek to hinder you with thoughts of losing your independence and freedom. A true guide, however, will never seek to limit these things. The guide will only take you as far as you are willing to go. On this path, it is your choices that determine your destination. Bad choices will hinder you; good choices will elevate you. Surrendering your choice will take you into unending depth.

"Those who continue to fight the self with positivity will eventually reach the pinnacle of spiritual enlightenment. This is the meaning behind our saying that the one who considers everyone but himself a friend of the Divine is himself a friend of the Divine. This is where the third blow to the self occurs, and the third stage begins."

Another student asked:

"How can one tell if what he feels is from the Attributes of the Divine or from himself?"

He said:

"Let's take anger as an example. There is human anger and Divine Anger. People invoke Divine Anger when they move deeper into negativity and harm themselves or others. We also see people harming others and getting angry. The difference between the two is that we are quick to express our anger and take it out on others, whereas the Divine remains silent. There is no Divine Punishment every time someone does something wrong. It means He gives chances despite wrongdoing and is quick to forgive. This is why the Beloved Nabi Pak ﷺ tells us that the Almighty says, 'My Mercy predominates My Wrath.' So, for those who have reached the peak of spiritual enlightenment, if they experience anger and are quick to express it, then that anger comes from themselves, or even from the devil. If they are silent and forbearing, then it is definitely from the Creator."

A student asked:

"People who have attained spiritual

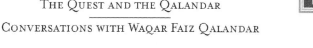
enlightenment can still be approached by the devil?"

He replied:

"If the devil comes in our way, it is the best way to know that we are going on the right path. The deeper you go, the more he will try to ambush you. The ones closest to the Divine are the ones most pursued by the devil. The devil wants to extinguish the Divine light, and he knows that he cannot compete with the Divine, so he goes after the Divine servants instead, where the light of the Divine is brightest and most abundant. The friends of the Divine, however, do not even give him a second thought. They are actually happy that he comes after them, for his pursuit is proof of the Creator's presence."

He continued:

"Remember that spiritual enlightenment is but the first of many stages the seeker will experience on his journey toward the Divine. There is a difference between knowing through positivity and knowing through friendship. It is after the third blow to the self that friendship can begin."

Another student asked:

"The example you gave seems to suggest that a friend of the Divine can still experience some resistance from the self."

He smiled and said:

"That is because the third blow does not actually annihilate the self. The final blow to the self does not come about through any action of the seeker but by the Action of the Divine Himself. In the first three blows, the seeker started removing the veils that stand between him and the Divine. These veils are made by the self, and when they are removed, friendship with the Divine begins. However, the Divine also has His own veils in place. The final blow to the self happens when the Divine removes those veils and unveils His Essence to His friend. There is no method or process to ensure such a thing happens. It is purely at the discretion of the Divine. This is the point where our love stops, and His special love begins."

The same student asked:

"Is there really no other way for this annihilation of self to happen?"

His smile grew wider as he said:

"The only other way is to be linked to someone who already has this relationship with the Divine. If your spiritual guide is someone beloved to the Divine in this way, then for the sake of that Divine Love, the Divine will remove the self from you as well. Recognizing this quality in a spiritual guide is the absolute purest form of positivity and guarantees spiritual victory against the self."

THE DEEPER YOU DELVE INTO WISDOM, THE MORE YOU WILL FIND YOURSELF SEEKING THE DIVINE. THOSE WHOSE SOULS ARE ENLIGHTENED WITH WISDOM WILL SURELY FIND THEIR CREATOR.

THE NINTH

KNOWLEDGE & WISDOM

Murshid was once sitting with some visitors who had come to ask about the spiritual path.

One of them asked:

"Are there any books we can read to gain knowledge of the Sufi path?"

He replied:

"There are many books that can be read, but very little of what you read will give you any benefit."

The same visitor asked:

"Why were these books written if they are not of any benefit?"

He replied:

"Most of these books were written by spiritual guides for their students to provide them instruction on their spiritual journeys. Their words sometimes hold some guidance for others on their spiritual search or even their spiritual journey, but to those who are not seeking the path, the words will just be another veil between them and their Lord.

"There are many who read books and arrive at the precipice of reaching the Divine, but then their incomplete knowledge gives rise to arrogance, and they turn away from Him at the last second. They mistakenly believe that everything there is to know about the subject is in the books they read. Nothing could be further from the truth. Sufism is a term for acting, not for knowing. This path is meant to be walked on, to be experienced."

He continued:

"We have been given a lot of time on this earth, but if we take out the time needed for our basic necessities, our obligations, and responsibilities, have very little free time left. If we use that little free time to simply read about a path that is meant to be enacted, then we are surely wasting what time we have. Sufism is not the path of knowledge, but the path of wisdom."

Another visitor asked: "What is the difference between knowledge and wisdom?"

He replied: "Knowledge will teach you what to say. Wisdom will teach you when to say it. Knowledge will inform you of the tangible world, whereas wisdom will inform you of the unseen world. Knowledge leads you to speak, whereas wisdom teaches you to listen. Knowledge expands the mind, whereas wisdom expands the heart. Knowledge will teach you to say, 'This is mine, and that is yours,' whereas wisdom will teach you to say, 'What's mine is yours too.' Knowledge brings you closer to created things, whereas wisdom brings you closer to the Creator.

"Bear in mind that when we say knowledge, we mean incomplete knowledge, which is knowledge without practice. Complete knowledge will always lead you to the wellsprings of wisdom. Incomplete knowledge will become just another burden to carry. If we have knowledge that we cannot implement, then that knowledge will certainly do more harm than good, and knowledge of the path cannot be implemented if one is not actually on the path."

Another visitor asked:

"If knowledge is found in books, then where is wisdom found?"

He smiled and said:

"On the path of knowledge, one drinks from the fountain of literature. On the path of wisdom, one drinks from the gaze of his guide. Wisdom comes directly from the Divine, and the medium will always be one's spiritual guide. Before finding a guide, one does gain wisdom, but the difference between the wisdom gained without a guide and that gained with a guide is like the difference between a pool and a thousand oceans."

Another visitor asked:

"If incomplete knowledge is a burden and a veil, then what does complete knowledge do for us on the path?"

He replied:

"Your spirituality begins with but a single step. Complete knowledge will give you what you need to take that step. Once the doors of wisdom are opened to you, you start to fly. Knowledge, complete knowledge, certainly has its place on this path. Nabi Pak Muhammad ﷺ once said, 'I am the city of knowledge, and Ali is its door.' He also said, 'I am the house of wisdom, and Ali is its door.' The source of complete knowledge and wisdom is the same. Complete knowledge will show you a path, but you must walk the path once it is shown to you. This is where wisdom begins."

Another visitor asked:

"Is it right to gain wisdom simply for the sake of gaining it?"

He replied:

"Seeking wisdom to gain wisdom is foolish. Searching for anything that will take you away from the Divine, even if that thing is wisdom, is foolish. If you truly want to seek wisdom, seek the Divine, and wisdom will bow before you at every step. When you are on the path of seeking the Divine, the Ultimate Source, you will find wisdom scattered about you like pebbles on a path."

"Both knowledge and wisdom, if gained for the

sake of anything other than the Divine, will lead you to disaster. With no place to direct that knowledge and wisdom, it becomes attached to the self. The problem always arises when we put ourselves before Him. Many practitioners of spirituality have fallen prey to this pitfall. Those who seek wisdom and not the Divine will find a world of hurt and heartbreak. Those who are guided to the Divine will find wisdom chasing after them."

The same visitor said:
"If someone who has spent his life gaining incomplete knowledge wants to switch to gaining wisdom, what should he do?"

He replied:
All one has to do is take any one thing he has knowledge of and practice it with total devotion. The love that arises from that practice will open the doors of wisdom to him. The Almighty will surely open a path to him that will lead him to spirituality."

A student present in the gathering asked:
"What is the ultimate level of wisdom?"

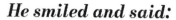
He smiled and said:

"The ultimate level is reached when one realizes that there is no ultimate level. The Divine is unlimited, and if the source is unlimited, then it will continue to provide wisdom. The mind has a limit to how much knowledge it can attain, but the heart is the abode of the Divine light. It is as vast as the Divine Throne itself, and it can become vaster still."

He paused for a moment and continued:

"The oceans of wisdom one attains from one's guide are in reality drops that spill from what the master himself is receiving. The most a student can get from his master is a drop. To get lost in this one drop is the ultimate form of wisdom for the seeker."

Return, no matter how often you lose your way. With more love than a mother waiting for her child, the Divine waits for you.

THE TENTH DIALOGUE

PURITY

The master once held a gathering for students and visitors, and during this gathering, he brought up the concept of purity.

He said:

"Our Master, the Beloved Nabi ﷺ once said that purity is a secret that Allah bestows to the hearts of those whom He loves."

A visitor interjected:

"People claim to love Allah, and they worship Him in private and public. Is this the key to attaining that love?"

He smiled and replied:

"Allah certainly already loves us immensely. He loves each human more than seventy mothers. However, the love that we are speaking of is on a different level. This level of love is bestowed to those who seek Him or those whom He seeks. We certainly make claims of His love, and He certainly hears these proclamations that we make on our tongues and in our hearts. However, you should know that when someone makes these claims, the Almighty will always look deep into his heart to see how true these claims he makes really are. Only when that purity is confirmed in the heart does the Divine make space in it for His love and secrets.

"Even before you embark on this path, the purity of your intention determines your destination."

A student asked him:

"What is the true definition of this purity?"

He answered:

"When a person does not even notice his own worship when even the acts of kindness he hides from others become hidden from himself when the words on his tongue are the same as the feelings of his heart, then this is the start of that purity. The start point of this purity is when he does not notice his own worship or good deeds; his gaze is fixed firmly on the Divine. This is when he can become a traveler on this path.

"Remember, the only distance between you and your destination is the purity of your intention. Hence, purity is the foundation stone of this path."

A visitor said:

"I'm still confused about what exactly purity is."

The Master replied:

"Let me give you a simple example. Let's say that your spouse invites his friends over for the evening and asks you to make an elaborate dish for dinner. You spend the entire day procuring the ingredients and preparing the dish. At the last minute, just before the guests are due to arrive, you accidentally overcook the dish and burn it. In a state of panic, you call your mother, but she lives in a different city, so she cannot help you. If you tell your spouse, he will immediately tell all of his friends and scold you. At such a moment like this, when you have no one to turn to, when you turn to Allah and call out to Him from your heart, the feeling you experience in that moment is purity!"

Another student asked:
"What is impurity?"

He said:
"If you did something good and you still remember it, that's impurity, for if good deeds are done purely for Him, then you would not remember them.

"So, if your own good deeds come between you and your Lord, then the self becomes involved, and this is the essence of impurity."

A visitor asked:
"How can we know whether or not our hearts are pure?"

He smiled and said:
"The one who is pure will never dwell on whether he is pure or not. He will always assume he is not pure and strive to be better."

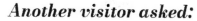

Another visitor asked:

"As one moves further along on the spiritual path, what kind of role does purity play?"

He answered:

"The greatest and most beautiful of our secrets is the purity of our intention. Acts of kindness should not be done to seek praise from people but to seek His friendship. When our actions begin to be purely done with the intention to please Him and Him Alone, He bestows our hearts with greater purity and His Divine Secrets. This purity, in turn, allows us to dive further into the depths of the spiritual path. Each level of depth requires a greater level of purity, and when we have the determination to stay on this path, the Almighty opens the purity up to us."

Another visitor asked:

"We often want to show purity and walk the path of the Divine, but then we are reminded of our past misdeeds, and we think we will never be able to get past them. How can we move forward when these misdeeds of our past weigh down on us?"

He said:

"The key is repentance. It is only repentance that

has the power to purify our hearts. His Mercy lies in our repentance and His forgiveness. If He accepts our repentance, He enriches our hearts with His Divine love so much that there is no room left for anything else, much less depression over the past or anxiety over the future.

"The word 'forgiveness' is purely for those who do wrong, both intentionally and unintentionally. This tells us that the people who do wrong are actually much more valuable to the Almighty. A mother is always worried about a child who is weak or lost. How, then, can He, who loves us seventy times more than a mother, ever leave us alone and unforgiven? All we need to do is know our flaws, own our mistakes and ask for forgiveness with the purest intention."

Another visitor asked:
"Sometimes we perceive impurity from others and are hurt by that. How do we deal with the impurity of others?"

He replied:
"True purity is to turn your attention to the Divine and away from the actions of others. The Divine is the One who heals, and your purity will

eventually be a source of healing not only for yourself but for others."

Another student said:
"We show purity for the sake of Allah, but people call us fools because of it."

Murshid asked:
"What do you do that makes people call you fools?"

The student replied:
"We give things away in the Name of Allah, and when people see this, they ridicule us."

He said:
"Subhanallah, is it not amazing to have someone call you a fool in the Name of Allah? Is it not amazing to be called a fool in the name of the Beloved Nabi ﷺ? Is it not amazing to experience hardship in the Name of Allah, to be forgiven in the Name of Allah? When the Name of Allah becomes involved, then the people of Allah welcome all negative and positive experiences with smiles on their faces. Why would we hesitate to be called fools in the Name of Allah? Is Allah not watching what is being done in His Name?

Does He not know the level of purity with which we act? Is there anything that the people of Allah are cognizant of other than Allah Himself? This is also a part of purity."

Another student asked:
"Does Allah show any kind of purity toward us?"

He replied:
"Look at the blessings you have been given and look at your own record of deeds and misdeeds. We continue to slip up and disobey Him, but does He not still bestow blessings on us? He gives to us without any expectation. This is His purity. Consider those who completely reject Him. Do they not eat of the same earth, drink of the same water, breathe of the same air? This is His purity.

"Another level of Allah's purity is when He accepts our purity and begins sharing His Divine Secrets. What is a secret? It is something someone tells only to you purely based on your friendship with him. A secret is not given in exchange for something else; it is given simply because one is present. When these Divine Secrets begin to unfold in the heart of man, he is taken into a different world entirely, a new world of purity where he truly sees no one other than the Divine.

"The ultimate level of purity, known only to a few, is where the Divine makes you His sole focus. He is the Almighty, His Attention is everywhere, but when He Himself becomes an ardent lover, He reserves His special Gaze and Attention just for that one beloved. The affairs of the universe become business as usual, and His personal work becomes the work of this beloved. The actions of people going about their daily business are recompensed in the Afterlife, whereas the actions of even the people engaged in the business of that beloved of the Divine are recompensed immediately, both in this life and the next. The ultimate purity of the One will always be for one."

LOYALTY IS TO SURRENDER YOUR OWN BEING AND ACCEPT HIS BEING.

THE ELEVENTH DIALOGUE

LOYALTY

Murshid was once seated in a gathering when a visitor asked:

"Why is loyalty so important on this path?"

He said:

"To understand loyalty, we must first understand the concept of idol worship, its history, and how it came about.

"When the Almighty created Adam, He commanded the angels to prostrate to him. Everyone prostrated except Satan. Satan was once a great worshipper of the Divine, so why this sudden change of attitude? The reason was that Satan considered himself superior. The reason Satan did not bow was jealousy. He was jealous that the Divine light was placed in a creature made of clay, whereas he was made of fire, but that Divine light was not given to him.

"The Divine has selected man as His representative. The ones specially selected to convey His message to the world have been and will always be humans. A person can see the signs of the Creator in this world and conclude that the Divine exists, but in order to receive actual correspondence from the Divine, we need his messengers. This has been the work of every prophet and messenger from Adam to Nabi Pak Muhammad ﷺ, and after the ending of prophethood, that work was entrusted to the friends of the Divine starting with Hazrat Ali. The Divine light has been placed in humanity. There are qualities in humans that give us hints as to the qualities of the Divine. We cannot truly know the Divine without knowing his human representative. This is the system of the Almighty, and to reject this system is to show disloyalty to Him, which is why Satan was cast out.

"Satan branded himself not as an enemy to the Divine, but an enemy to humanity. There can be no competition or victory against the Almighty, so the only other option is to have a conflict with His representatives. Mankind is made of clay, given life through the Divine act of creation, and given a special status due to the special Divine light placed within him. Satan tries to copy this by making his own clay statues and putting his own machinations behind them. This is the origin of idol worship. The origin of idol worship, then, is disloyalty to the Divine. Therefore, the first level of loyalty is to eschew all forms of idol worship."

Another visitor asked:
"All forms of idol worship? Isn't idol worship to bow to statues instead of the Divine?"

He replied:
"Idols are made by people. People make idols both on the earth and in the heart. Turning away from the physical idols is the first level of loyalty. When you first accept the path of Nabi Pak Muhammad ﷺ, it requires that you accept

105

only the One as your sole object of worship. The second level of loyalty only occurs after accepting this path. You have already accepted the One as your sole Lord, but now you take your loyalty deeper and start to break the idols kept in your heart. As the seeker removes these idols, his heart is able to take in more and more of the Divine light. Remembrance of the Divine begins to become prominent in his mind and heart."

The same visitor asked:
"What are these inner idols?"

He replied:
"Your own desires. The desires we keep in our hearts that pervade our thoughts and serve as the reasons for our actions are the idols of the heart. The seeker at the first stage of loyalty has turned away from physical idols, but these inner idols still keep him occupied."

Another visitor asked:
"What kind of desires? Are there desires that are permitted?"

He replied:
"There are certain desires that are impermissible.

These have been laid out by Nabi Pak Muhammad
ﷺ. The seeker at the second level of loyalty
removes these desires from his heart. There
are also certain desires that are permissible.
The seeker reaches the third level of loyalty by
removing even those from the heart. At the third
level of loyalty, the seeker pledges his whole
being to the Divine and gives up even that which
is praiseworthy purely for His sake. He no longer
seeks reward for his good works; he seeks only
the Divine Essence."

Another visitor asked: "How does one know when
one is distracted by worldly desires?"

He replied:

"The world is anything that takes you away
from the Divine. There are many things people
engage with in their daily affairs, like their
career, their ambitions, or their short-term goals.
These things often serve as distractions. There
are some people, however, who understand
that these things are all necessities of life and
engage with them as such. They do not indulge
in these things for themselves but rather for the
sake of the Divine. These things are no longer
distractions for them. Then there are some people
who engage in spiritual activities but only do

so for their own benefit. These exercises were designed to bring one closer to the Divine, but these people misuse them and forget about the Divine instead. For such people, these spiritual exercises are distractions. So, if what you are engaged in, whatever it may be, is bringing you closer to the Divine, then your loyalty is getting deeper. If it is taking you away from the Divine, then it is a distraction."

The visitor who first spoke said:
"I still don't understand the connection between loyalty and idol worship, or why loyalty is so important."

He said:
"My master Hazrat Ali says, 'Whenever I can grasp a concept in my mind, I know that it is not Allah.' The Divine always defines Himself as what He is not, not as what He is. This is because whenever you focus your attention on something assuming it to be the Divine, the Divine will not be found there. The minute you try to define the Divine as something, it becomes an idol. The Prophet Abraham looked first to the stars, then the Moon, then the Sun, but could not find the Divine in any of them. Then he proclaimed that

he turned his face not to anything created but to the One who created everything. This is the essence of loyalty. Without loyalty, we cannot begin even to recognize the Divine Essence, much less reach Him."

Another visitor asked:

"Isn't wanting to reach the Divine itself a desire?"

He smiled and said:

"Yes, it is. At the third level of loyalty, the seeker gives up permissible desires. This is where the Divine will bestow upon him His authority. Miracles can manifest at this stage. The seeker uses this authority with the permission of the Almighty. This is the loyalty of the friends of the Divine. At the fourth level of loyalty, the seeker gives up even spiritual desires. These desires pertain to the goal, like reaching a level of friendship with the Divine or reaching a particular place in closeness to the Divine. At the fifth level, the seeker gives up even the desire of the Divine. Here is where the seeker's activity stops, and the Divine's activity begins. The first four stages involved the seeker moving forward while the Divine watched. At the fifth stage, the seeker simply watches the Action of the

Divine. This is the stage where countless aspects of the Divine are revealed to the seeker, and his acceptance of these aspects form the completion of his loyalty. He sees the system of the Divine, the actions of the Divine, the pleasure of the Divine, and keeps his own will in accordance with all of that. He gives up even the authority that the Divine bestowed upon him. This is the loyalty of the close friends of the Divine."

A student asked:

"You have given examples of people who showed loyalty. Is there any example of people who showed this highest loyalty?"

He replied:

"The Ahl-ul-Bayt, the family of the Noble Messenger ﷺ. They showed a level of loyalty even higher than this in their actions and decisions. Their example will be cited at the ultimate loyalty until the end of time."

Another student asked:

"Is there any chance for someone to find the same type of loyalty?"

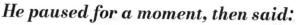

He paused for a moment, then said:

"The seeker is one who shows loyalty to the Divine. The Divine Himself will always show greater loyalty to His beloved. Loyalty from man comes in stages. Loyalty from the Divine comes to His beloved raw, unfiltered, and beyond time. The beloved of the Divine will receive the sole loyalty of the Creator. If a seeker can find such a beloved of the Divine and show loyalty to that person, he can traverse the stages of loyalty in a single night."

THE MURSHID IS SOMEONE WHO IS DIVINELY GUIDED, THE ONE WHO SHOWS YOU THE WAY—THE WAY THAT LEADS YOU TO THE ONE WHO CREATED YOU.

THE TWELFTH DIALOGUE

THE MURSHID & THE MUREED

Some people pondering the path came across a few questions about the nature of a spiritual guide and the need for a guide to reach the goal. They once came to visit the master and presented him with these questions.

They asked:

"What exactly is the role of the spiritual guide?"

He replied:

"Most people ponder about the role of a Murshid, the spiritual guide, when they should be concerned with the role of the seeker. Until one understands the role of the disciple, one can never understand the role of the master."

He continued:

"The path of Sufism is based purely on the master-disciple relationship. The experience of the Divine is given from heart to heart. Without this heart connection, one might be able to experience something of the Divine, but he will not be able to experience everything that the Divine has to offer him."

One of them asked:

"Why is it that there can only be one connection?"

He smiled and said:

"There is only one Creator. Your journey starts with one and ends with one. The One will always set one for you by whom you will reach that One. Understanding that it is the Creator who has kept your spiritual sustenance in the hands of one person is the first step to understanding His Oneness."

Another visitor asked:

"Does that mean we cannot learn from other people?"

He replied:

"As long as a seeker is on his journey to the Divine, he will find that he learns from nearly every person he meets. He will sit with the unlikeliest people and gain wisdom and insight. The question is where this insight comes from. A true seeker will find that the words come from the mouth of a person, but the meaning behind those words is unveiled to him by his guide, even if that guide is not physically present."

Another visitor asked:

"What exactly is a seeker's goal?"

He said:

"A seeker is simply one who seeks the Divine, anyone with an urge to seek out the Almighty. Those who follow this compulsion will find themselves walking toward the path of spirituality. His quest will take on many phases that will seem like journeys to him. Eventually, if he is pure and persistent in his quest, he will be guided by the Divine to his Murshid. This is when his journey to the Divine truly begins. He takes the hand of his Murshid and becomes his student, a Mureed, meaning one who has will. He chooses this path by his own will and makes the best use out of everything he has gained on his quest, implementing it to get closer to the Almighty."

Another visitor asked:

"If the quest is spiritual and not physical, then can't the Murshid also be spiritual and not physical?"

He replied:

"The quest is at its root spiritual, but it takes place in this life, and so it is also physical. We still inhabit these physical bodies, and as long as we do, our Murshid will have to be in the physical world with a physical body. The Murshid is meant to take us from the purely physical world to the realm of the spiritual. He teaches us how the physical and spiritual are interconnected, as well as how they are separate. The Murshid teaches how to improve spiritually while navigating life physically."

He continued:

"Every master was once himself a student. There is an unbroken chain of masters that leads back to Hazrat Ali, the Penultimate Master of Spirituality, and from there the chain ends at

Nabi Pak Muhammad ﷺ."

Another visitor asked:
"We know how a person becomes a Mureed, but how does one become a Murshid?"

He replied:
"A seeker becomes a guide at the sole discretion of the Murshid. The Murshid determines who is ready to help others. However, only a Mureed who is Kamil, complete, is capable of taking on this responsibility."

The same visitor asked:
"What happens after someone becomes a Murshid?"

He smiled and said:
"Becoming a Murshid does not mean one's spiritual journey ends. For someone who is made into a Murshid, a totally new phase of his journey begins. As he guides others, his guidance from the Divine also increases. New aspects of the spiritual path open up to him until finally, he reaches the state of becoming a Kamil Murshid."

The same visitor asked:
"What happens after that?"

He replied:
"The stage of being a Kamil Murshid is something given by the Creator. One cannot reach it by his own effort. After this stage, if the Almighty wants to take such a person deeper, he will continue to move forward. One of the highest levels of this stage is when someone receives guidance from Hazrat Ali, the master of masters."

He chuckled softly and continued:
"The stages of completion of a Murshid are not recorded anywhere, nor are they easy to understand. No one who ever reached those stages was ever concerned with becoming a Murshid. They made their sole purpose becoming a Kamil Mureed."

A visitor asked:
"What is a Kamil Mureed?"

He said:
"A Kamil Mureed is one who, after taking on the spiritual path at the hands of his Murshid,

remains firm and determined on that path. He absorbs the teachings of his Murshid like a sponge and holds fast to those teachings, staying in the service of his guide. This is the path opted for by the friends of the Divine. Books have been filled with stories of how they served their masters when they were students for years on end. A Kamil Mureed is someone who shows loyalty to his Murshid."

Another visitor asked:

"What happens if a Mureed turns away from his Murshid on his spiritual journey?"

He replied:

"When the Divine wishes to bestow you with a connection to Him that is truly unique to you, He will place all of your spiritual sustenance in the hands of your Murshid. If you turn away from those hands, you are turning away from the very source of your spirituality. This is the one action that will stop your spiritual progression in its tracks. On this path, stopping is akin to falling. It is like throwing a ball in the air. The second it stops, you know it is about to fall back down. The connection between a Murshid and a Mureed, however, is everlasting. As long as the

Mureed turns back, he will always be able to walk the spiritual path."

The same visitor asked:
"I have heard that some seekers are selected by the Divine to walk the spiritual path."

He replied:
"Yes, that is true. There are two types of students: Mureed and Murad. A Mureed is someone who chooses to be on this path. A Murad is someone preselected by the Divine to be on this path. A Murad can experience in days what a Mureed will experience in years. These types of people are very few in relation to Mureeds. Despite all of their favors, however, if they turn away from the Murshid, they will experience the same result as a Mureed who turns away. This seldom happens for a Murad, though, for a true Murad is like a reflection of his Murshid."

The visitors paused, unsure of what to say next.

He smiled and said:
"The path begins and ends with a single step. The Divine gives us all that we need, and the

rest of the path is spent realizing what we have been given. Be it a Mureed or a Murad, the one who realizes that he has gained everything from the gaze of his Murshid has reached the depths of spirituality."

TRUE APPRECIATION
AND ACCEPTANCE OF
THE CREATOR COME
WHEN YOU HAVE NO ONE
ELSE TO TURN TO.

126

THE THIRTEENTH DIALOGUE

SUPPLICATION

The master was once sitting with some people, and the subject of supplication arose.

One student asked him:

"What is the importance of supplication?"

He replied:

"Supplication is one of the basic ways to connect with the Divine. Supplication is to plead with the Divine. We plead with someone when we feel we have a need. Despite all the blessings the Creator has given us, we fail to communicate with him using those blessings. When we feel an emptiness, a void, when we feel that something is missing, then we plead with our Creator to fill that void. Humans tend to have animalistic habits that lead them to look at what they do not have instead of what they do have. The Creator, in His Mercy, has made supplication the basic line of communication between Him and us so that we call out to him in those times when we feel that emptiness. When this line of communication is opened and used frequently, we start to notice the seen and unseen blessings He has kept scattered around us. Our animalistic habits change into true human nature, and our perspective broadens. Supplication is the key to opening the channels of spirituality in our hearts."

A *visitor asked*:

"Isn't supplication just asking for things? I thought the Sufi was supposed to avoid material things."

He replied:

"Supplication has levels. The first level is asking for things to fill the void that we feel. We may or may not get what we asked for, but in the moment we call out to Him, we definitely receive some spiritual sustenance."

A visitor said:

"Some people get frustrated when they don't get what they want, and they give up praying altogether. Why doesn't the Divine answer some supplications, even if they are made from a place of desperation?"

He replied:

"If a five-year-old boy asks for a motorcycle, his parents or guardians will definitely not give it to him. In about twenty years, maybe they will honor that request. The Divine loves more than seventy mothers. He will only bestow a blessing you ask for if and when you are ready for it. If a supplication you made is not being realized, then you must have confidence that it will happen at the right time."

A visitor asked:

"If the Creator has written what we will receive in our destinies, then why ask for it at all?"

He replied:

"Perhaps it is written that it will only reach you when you ask for it."

The same visitor asked:

"If He already knows what we want, then why ask for it?"

He replied: "When you sit on a park bench and look at the ground beneath the trees, the sunlight shines through on parts of the ground. All the ground is equally visible to you, but the parts where the Sun is falling shine the most. This is the difference between those who ask and those who do not. The ones who do not ask are the shaded parts of the ground, and the ones who do are the patches shining in the Sun. All are equally visible to the Divine, but the ones who call out to Him shine the most. It is less about receiving what you ask for and more about receiving His attention. When someone realizes this, he moves on to the next level of supplication.

"The second level of supplication is where someone stops asking simply for material things and starts asking for spiritual things. He will ask for closeness to the Divine or even to be put on the spiritual path. Someone at this level will also excessively recite salutations upon the Noble Messenger ﷺ. One who consistently does this is guided to his Murshid, and his level of supplication deepens. As he follows the path under the guidance of his Murshid, he eventually moves from the second level to the third level.

"The third level of supplication is that of a Kamil Mureed. He supplicates not to ask of the Divine but to plead and show obeisance to Him. Having recognized the immense favors of the Divine upon him with the help of his Murshid, he stays bent in humility and gratitude toward the Divine. He begins to submit himself to his Lord. As his submission increases, so too does his love and longing for the Divine. This is when he reaches the fourth level.

"The fourth level of supplication is when the seeker seeks Divine blessings for others and the Divine Essence for himself. This is a type of supplication that is very pleasing to the Divine. He is quick to accept supplications made for others. Because His response is quick, the communication channel between the seeker and the Divine becomes deeper and stronger. His submission takes on a new level of purity. The seeker begins to perceive the presence of the Divine. When this perception fully develops, he reaches the fifth level.

"The fifth level of supplication is where the seeker does not ask or plead in his supplications; rather, he supplicates simply to communicate with the Divine. This is the supplication of a friend of the Almighty."

One visitor asked:
"Isn't this just like a conversation, then?"

He smiled and replied:
"Yes, it is. Think of the last time you called a friend. You let out all of your emotions and shared all your experiences, and your friend listened to everything. This is how the friends of the Divine are as well. They speak to the Divine in supplication just as we speak to our friends over the phone. They do not speak to ask; they speak simply to converse. A seeker who goes deep into this level will stop communicating with words and start communicating with tears and silence. His relationship with the Divine reaches a point where he does not need words to convey anything to Him."

A student asked:
"What about the Divine? If supplication becomes a conversation, then shouldn't He say something too?"

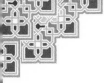

Murshid's smile grew wide as he said:
"This is the final level of supplication, where
the friend is silent, and the Divine speaks.
This is the supplication of the knowers of the
Almighty, the closest friends of the Divine.
The Divine will unveil His words to them, and
they listen. A good friend is a good listener,
so their listening extends past creation and to
the Creator. They will hear the Creator in their
moments of silence as well as when others speak.
It reaches a point where the only thing they can
hear is the Creator."

Some Wise
Waqar Faiz

SAYINGS OF QALANDAR

THE DESIRE TO FIND THE CREATOR COMES FROM NO ONE BUT YOURSELF.

WE HAVE PLENTY OF INTELLECTUAL
POWER. WHAT WE NEED MORE OF IS
SPIRITUAL POWER.

AN ARTIST BECOMES INSPIRED BY
NATURE AND ITS COLORS, AND THAT
IS HOW HE CREATES A BEAUTIFUL
PAINTING WITH A BALANCED
COMPOSITION. WHY SHOULDN'T
THE REST OF US TAKE INSPIRATION
FROM NATURE WHEN WE PAINT OUR
RELATIONSHIPS AND LIFE GOALS?
WE DEFY NATURE AND ITS BEAUTY;
HENCE WE SUFFER.

THE MORE YOU SEEK THE DIVINE,
THE MORE YOU KNOW THAT YOU
ARE NOT FOR THIS WORLD. RATHER,
THE WORLD IS FOR YOU, AND YOU
ARE FOR HIM.

YOUR JOURNEY TO YOUR CREATOR
IS DETERMINED BY THE VASTNESS OF
YOUR HEART.

It is not about how much you claim to love Him. It is about how consistent and exclusive your love is for Him.

WE DON'T THINK TWICE WHEN IT
COMES TO RECEIVING, SO WHY DO
WE HAVE SECOND THOUGHTS WHEN
IT COMES TO GIVING?

LIVE IN THIS WORLD, BUT DON'T LET THIS WORLD LIVE IN YOU. YOU WILL FIND THINGS POSSESSING PEOPLE RATHER THAN PEOPLE POSSESSING THINGS. THE WORLD IS YOUR POSSESSION, AND DON'T FORGET THAT YOU ARE HIS POSSESSION.

GIVE TO YOUR HEART DEPTH AS THE SEA. FOR COUNTLESS RIVERS COME AND MEET WITHIN THE SEA, AND YET IT DOES NOT BECOME FULL.

THERE IS A DIFFERENCE BETWEEN
GIVING AND SERVING. IT DOES NOT
MATTER HOW MUCH YOU GIVE;
WHAT MATTERS IS HOW MUCH LOVE
YOU GIVE IT WITH.

THE BEST THING YOU CAN DO IS
MAKE A MISTAKE, AND THE WORST
THING YOU CAN DO IS BE ARROGANT
ABOUT THAT MISTAKE.

You cannot be friends with the Divine if you don't take from what He has given you and pay it forward for His sake.

EVERY HARDSHIP IS AN
OPPORTUNITY TO SHED A LAYER
OF YOURSELF, AND EVERY LAYER
SHED LEADS TO A DIVINE LAYER
UNVEILED.

PLACE YOUR EXPECTATIONS FROM OTHERS IN THE COURT OF THE ALMIGHTY, AND THE DOORS OF RELIEF WILL BE OPENED TO YOU.

IF YOU ARE NOT KIND TO CREATION,
YOU CAN NEVER FIND THE
CREATOR, FOR THE CLOSER YOU ARE
TO THEM, THE CLOSER YOU ARE TO
HIM.

If you want to know if your Lord is pleased with you, ask yourself: Are you pleased with Him?

WHEN YOU ARE SILENT, THE DIVINE
SPEAKS.

THE EXPANSIVENESS OF THE HEART
DETERMINES HOW MUCH DIVINE
LOVE YOU RECEIVE.

We know that seeking God will lead us to Him, and seeking the world will lead us away from Him. The journey itself informs us of our destination.

DETERMINATION IS NOT JUST HAVING FIRM FEET. IT IS HAVING ONE FOOT FIRMLY ON THE GROUND AND THE OTHER RAISED, READY FOR THE NEXT STEP IN YOUR JOURNEY.

THERE IS NO HOPELESSNESS FOR THE FRIENDS OF THE DIVINE.

SEEKERS OF THE DIVINE MOVE
FROM TEMPORARY JOY TO
PERPETUAL JOY.

HUMILITY IS CONSTANT
CONSIDERATION OF THE ONE WHO
IS GREATER THAN YOU.

THE BEST SERVICE TO THE DIVINE
IS SERVICE TO OTHERS.

THE MOST BEAUTIFUL PRAYER IS TO
SEEK HIS BLESSINGS FOR OTHERS
AND TO SEEK HIM FOR YOURSELF.

THE SENSE OF FULFILLMENT YOU GAIN FROM HELPING OTHERS IS GREATER THAN THE SENSE OF FULFILLMENT YOU GAIN FROM ANYTHING ELSE.

Service is never done for the pleasure of people. It is done for the sole pleasure of the Divine.

HOW CLOSE SOMEONE IS TO THE DIVINE CAN BE DISCERNED BY THEIR MANNERS IN DEALING WITH OTHERS—WHETHER THEY ARE SOFT AND SWEET WITH THEIR WORDS OR BITTER.

Service is never done for the pleasure of people. It is done for the sole pleasure of the Divine.

HOW CLOSE SOMEONE IS TO THE DIVINE CAN BE DISCERNED BY THEIR MANNERS IN DEALING WITH OTHERS—WHETHER THEY ARE SOFT AND SWEET WITH THEIR WORDS OR BITTER.

WISDOM SILENCES THE TONGUE
AND ENLIVENS THE HEART.

YOU SHOULD NOT FEAR THE DIVINE
BECAUSE OF PUNISHMENT. WHAT
YOU SHOULD FEAR IS HURTING
YOUR FRIENDSHIP WITH HIM

THE DIVINE LIGHT IS SO
WONDROUS; WHEREVER IT FINDS
SPACE, IT LEAVES NO ROOM FOR
ANYTHING ELSE.

LET NOT THE HEART BE RUSTED
BY OUR LIES. LET IT GLOW WITH
THE TRUTH, FOR SPEAKING THE
TRUTH REMOVES RUST FROM THE
HEART AND ILLUMINATES THE SOUL.

THE DIVINE HAS KEPT THE BEST
QUALITIES INSIDE EVERY HUMAN
BEING. WE NEED ONLY SEEK THEM
FROM WITHIN.

THE ULTIMATE EXAMPLE OF
LOYALTY COMES FROM THE
HOUSEHOLD OF THE MESSENGER
ﷺ. THEIR UNPRECEDENTED
FAITHFULNESS TO HIM SHALL BE
MENTIONED UNTIL THE END OF
TIME ITSELF. THEY ARE TRULY
THE SYMBOL OF FAITH, JUSTICE,
PERSEVERANCE, COURAGE, AND
SACRIFICE.

WISDOM IS A FRUIT THAT GROWS ON THE TREE OF PATIENCE. SO, IF WE WANT TO BE WISE, WE MUST LEARN TO BE PATIENT.

PATIENCE IS NOT HOW LONG YOU
WAIT. IT IS THE MANNER IN WHICH
YOU WAIT.

Divine light is with those who are patient. Do not react or respond in haste. Instead, choose silence and connect with Him. Let your response be guided by the Divine.

You will surely find the Divine with the brokenhearted.

THE ONLY DISTANCE BETWEEN
YOU AND YOUR DESTINATION IS
YOURSELF.

THE MAGNITUDE OF YOUR
SUBMISSION DETERMINES HOW
CLOSE THE DIVINE IS TO YOU.

SUBMISSION IS NOT SOMETHING
YOU HAVE TO DO. IT IS SOMETHING
YOU CHOOSE TO DO.

ENLIGHTENMENT IS TO SEE
THE FAULTS IN YOURSELF AND
PERFECTION IN OTHERS.

THE DIVINE CHOOSES HIS FRIENDS,

NOT PEOPLE.

THE PERFECTION OF SERVICE
LIES IN FORGETTING WHAT YOU
HAVE DONE FOR OTHERS AND
REMEMBERING WHAT OTHERS HAVE
DONE FOR YOU.

INNER PEACE LIES IN WORSHIP. THE
DIVINE LIES IN SERVICE.

IT IS THE GUIDE WHO CLEANSES YOUR HEART AND SHOWS YOU ITS REFLECTION OF THE DIVINE.

In pursuit of reaching the destination, don't forget to relish the journey.

BEAUTY STEMS NOT FROM
KNOWLEDGE POSSESSED BUT FROM
EXCELLENCE AND GOODNESS OF
CHARACTER.

Take but a single step forward with complete faith in Him, and the path will pave itself before you.

EVERYTHING MUST COME TO AN END. IT IS WHAT YOU DO BEFORE THIS MOMENT THAT WILL REMAIN FOREVER.

IMMERSE YOURSELF IN THE SERVICE OF CREATION, AND YOU WILL FIND YOURSELF CLOSEST TO THE CREATOR.

THIS LIFE HAS JUST ONE PURPOSE:
LOVE THE ONE WHO HAS CREATED
YOU AND EVERYTHING FOR YOU.

BE LIKE A TREE THAT PROVIDES
SHADE TO ALL WITHOUT
DISCRIMINATION.

You cannot create love; it blooms from a pure heart. If you seek love, then clean your heart and soften it so that the seed of love, when placed within, can give its fruit.

When you walk up a mountain, you bend forward and hunch your shoulders. When you walk down, you stiffen up so as not to slip. Similarly, when you are on an upward journey toward Him, you remain bent in submission. If you stiffen up in pride, it means you are on the way down.

NO ONE HAS SEEN HIM, YET
EVERYONE KNOWS OF HIM.

DIVINE FRIENDSHIP IS MADE WITH HIS ESSENCE, NOT WITH HIS ATTRIBUTES.

IF YOU LIKE SOMEONE A LOT, DO
NOT OBSERVE THEM TOO CLOSELY;
YOU MIGHT END UP FINDING FLAWS.

If you dislike someone, look at that person with an open heart and observe closely; you might find something beautiful.

IN MAGNITUDES, YOU CAN GIVE ALL
YOU WANT, BUT NONE OF IT WILL
MATTER UNTIL IT HAS COME FROM
THE HEART.

BE IT LITTLE BUT GIVEN WITH
LOVE—THIS IS WHAT IS MOST LOVED
BY HIM.

You should not fear the Divine because of punishment. What you should fear is hurting your friendship with Him

It is better to give before
you are asked to give.

HAVE COURAGE AND HEART. NIGHT FALLS, BUT IT IS ALWAYS FOLLOWED BY THE SUN, STARTING A NEW DAY, AND THEREFORE, A NEW HOPE.

A CLEVER MAN WILL SPEND HIS TIME
TRYING TO HAVE WHAT HE LIKES. A
WISE MAN WILL LIKE WHAT HE HAS.

To be happy is something wonderful. And even more wonderful still is when another's happiness is because of you.

AUTHORS WRITE WORDS ON PAPER.
FRIENDS OF THE DIVINE WRITE
WORDS ON THE HEAVENLY TABLET.

COURAGE IS GOING DEEP WITHIN
YOUR HEART AND FINDING THAT
SEED FROM WHICH YOU EXIST.

He awaits you with awe. Knowing this becomes your consistency.

YOUR COMPLAINT IS AN EXCUSE TO SHARE.

THERE IS BEAUTY IN WHAT IS
UNSEEN FROM THE EYES AND SEEN
FROM THE HEART.

YOU ARE WHO YOU ARE BECAUSE
YOU ARE LOVED.
ONE WHO REALIZES THIS HAS
FOUND ETERNAL COMPANIONSHIP.

IF YOU LOOK AT YOURSELF, YOU WILL FIND YOU ARE NOTHING. YOU LOOK AT HIM, YOU WILL FIND YOU ARE EVERYTHING.

COME TO TERMS WITH WHAT
ELUDES YOU SO THAT YOU CAN
ACCEPT WHAT LIES AHEAD OF YOU.

When love speaks, everything else remains silent.

IT IS NOT IN THE APPARENT THAT WE FIND THE DIVINE, BUT IN THE SUBTLE.

HEAR THE CRIES OF THE PEOPLE WHO HAVE NO ONE, AND YOU WILL FIND THE ONE WHO IS WITH EVERYONE.

SPIRITUALITY BEGINS WITH YOUR WILLINGNESS TO TAKE A STEP, AND IT ENDS WITH YOU TAKING THAT STEP.

Everyone asks Him for what they need, but only a few say, "How are you today?"

ACCEPTING THAT YOU ARE WRONG
IS THE LAST THING YOUR EGO
DESIRES.

THE FACT THAT YOUR HEART CAN
TURN IS THE REASON YOU ARE THE
GREATEST CREATION.

A SOUL DEEPLY CONNECTED TO
THE DIVINE WILL NEVER CEASE TO
WITNESS HIS WONDERS.

OUR BODIES MAY BE ASLEEP, BUT
THE SOUL'S JOURNEY NEVER STOPS.

GRATITUDE WHEN YOU'RE DOWN,
HUMBLENESS WHEN YOU'RE UP.

His Perfection is found in your
imperfection.

HIS GAZE ON WHAT BEATS WITHIN YOU MAKES IT A HEART. HIS ARRIVAL THERE MAKES IT HIS HOME.

YOUR GATEWAY TO THE DIVINE WILL ALWAYS BE THROUGH THE ONES THAT HE LOVES.

Made in the USA
Monee, IL
30 June 2022